Do I Have to Wear a Mask?

Written by
DeShawn Lavette Jones

Illustrated by
Glenn Jones

Dedication

To God's beautiful
rays of sunshine.

To all the healing
properties found in nature.
Nutrient-dense food.

I dig in my nose sometimes

Lightning Source UK Ltd.
Milton Keynes UK
UKHW050354050222
398248UK00002B/20